PRELIMINARY GRADE

Electric Guitar Playing

compiled by

Tony Skinner

on behalf of

RGT

Registry of Guitar Tutors

A CIP record for this publication is available from the British Library

ISBN 1-898466-50-5

Published in Great Britain by

REGISTRY PUBLICATIONS LTD

Registry Mews, 11 to 13 Wilton Road, Bexhill, Sussex, TN40 1HY

Music and text typesetting by

TakeNote Publishing Limited

54 Lincolns Mead, Lingfield, Surrey RH7 6TA

Printed and bound in Great Britain

Contents

Introduction

This handbook is primarily intended to give advice and information to candidates considering taking the Preliminary Grade examination in electric guitar playing, although undoubtedly it will be found that the information contained within will be helpful to all guitarists whether intending to take the examination or not.

GUITAROGRAPH

In order that scales and chords can be illustrated as clearly as possible, and made available for all to understand regardless of experience, notation and fingering are displayed via the use of the *guitarograph*.

The *guitarograph* uses a combination of tablature, traditional notation and fingerboard diagram – thereby ensuring clarity and leaving no doubt as to what is required. In the example shown above, all three notations refer to the same note, i.e. A on the 2nd fret of the 3rd (G) string, fretted with the 2nd finger. Each of the notation methods used in the *guitarograph* is explained below:

Tablature

The tablature is shown on the left of the guitarograph, with horizontal lines representing the strings (with the high E string being string 1), and the numbers on the string lines referring to the frets. A '0' on a line would mean play that string *open* (unfretted).

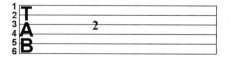

This means play at the second fret on the third string.

Musical notation

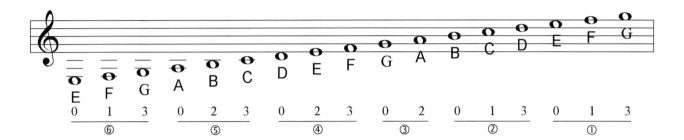

Notation on the treble clef is shown in the centre of the guitarograph.

A sharp (♯) before a note would raise its pitch by a semitone i.e. one fret higher, whilst a flat (♭) before a note would lower the pitch by a semitone, i.e. one fret lower. A natural sign (♮) before a note cancels a sharp or flat sign.

In the illustration above, the lower circled numbers refer to the string on which each note could be played, whilst the number immediately below each note indicates which fretting–hand finger could be used. The fingering is shown only to illustrate the exact pitch of each note.

Fingerboard diagram

The fingerboard diagram is shown on the right of the guitarograph with horizontal lines representing the strings. Vertical lines represent the frets, with fret numbers shown in Roman numerals. The numbers on the horizontal lines show the recommended fingering. Fingerings have been chosen which are likely to be the most effective for the widest range of players at this level, however there are a variety of alternative fingerings and fingerboard positions that could be used and you can use any other systematic fingerings that produce a good musical result.

This means play with the second finger at the second fret on the G string.

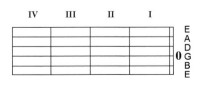

This means play the G string *open*, i.e. without fretting it.

Scale and chord spellings

Above each guitarograph is a scale or chord spelling. This lists the letter names of the notes within the scale or chord, together with their interval numbers. The interval numbers shown are based on their comparison to the major scale with the same starting pitch. The scale and chord spellings will help you identify the differences in construction between the various scales and chords, and will help you learn the names of the notes that you are playing.

For example:

			C major scale				
C	D	E	F	G	A	B	C
1	2	3	4	5	6	7	8

	C major chord	
C	E	G
1	3	5

ALTERNATIVE FINGERING

Whilst the notes indicated in the guitarographs are precise and definitive, the fingering given in all cases is only one possible recommended suggestion: any alternative systematic and effective fingerings will be acceptable. There is no requirement to use the exact fingerings shown within this book.

TUNING

The use of an electronic tuner or other tuning aid, *prior to, or at the start of the examination*, is permitted; candidates should be able to make any further adjustments, if required during the examination, unaided. The examiner will, upon request, offer an E or A note to tune to.

For examination purposes guitars should be tuned to Standard Concert Pitch (A=440Hz).

Candidates who normally tune to non-standard pitch (e.g. A=442Hz) should revert to Standard Concert Pitch for examination purposes. Candidates who normally tune a full tone or semitone higher/lower should either revert to Standard Pitch for the examination or should be prepared to transpose immediately upon request all requirements to Standard Pitch.

Scales

Here are the scales required for the Preliminary Grade examination.

C MAJOR SCALE – 1 OCTAVE

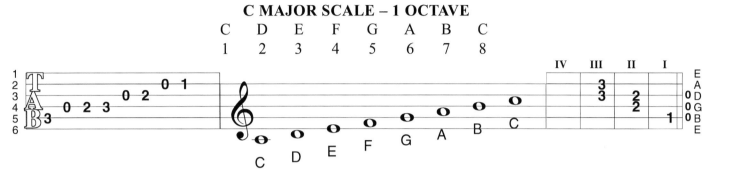

G PENTATONIC MAJOR SCALE – 1 OCTAVE

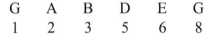

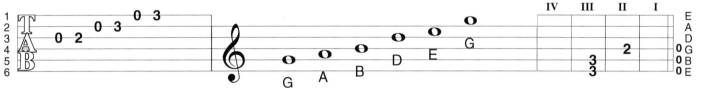

A NATURAL MINOR SCALE – 1 OCTAVE

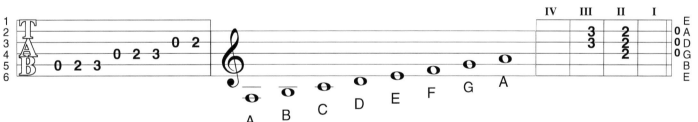

E BLUES SCALE – 1 OCTAVE

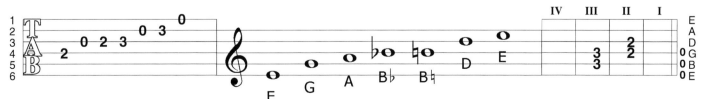

INFORMATION AND ADVICE

A maximum of 8 marks may be awarded in the 'scales' section of the examination.

The examiner may request you to play any of the required scales from memory. Each scale should be played once only, ascending and descending (i.e. from the lowest note to the highest and back again) without a pause and without repeating the top note.

Scales should be played at a tempo range of between 80 and 112 beats per minute. Choose a tempo at which you feel confident and comfortable and try to maintain this evenly throughout: evenness and clarity are more important than speed for its own sake.

Fretting-hand technique

Press the tips of the fretting-hand fingers as close to the fretwire as possible. This minimises buzzes and the amount of pressure required – enabling you to play with a lighter, clearer and hence more fluent touch.

Try to keep all the fretting-hand fingers close to the fingerboard, and have them ready to press in a 'hovering position', as this minimises the amount of movement required. Always have the fretting hand spread, with the fingers correctly spaced and ready in position hovering, before you start to play.

Picking-hand technique

Although it is not essential to use a plectrum (or pick) for this examination, you may find that not using one has a detrimental effect on speed, attack, volume and tone – or at least more effort will be required to achieve the same effect. However, the use of the fingers, rather than the plectrum, does offer greater flexibility. Ultimately the choice is personal. Both methods are acceptable, providing a strong clear tone is achieved.

If using a plectrum ensure to always alternate downstrokes with upstrokes. Grip the plectrum between the index finger and thumb. Position the plectrum so that its tip is just beyond the fingertip. If an excessive amount of plectrum tip extends beyond the finger a lack of pick control will result as the plectrum will flap around when striking the strings – this would consequently reduce fluency and accuracy. Be careful not to grip the plectrum too tightly as excessive gripping pressure can lead to muscular tension in the hand with subsequent loss of flexibility and movement.

Chords

Below are the chords required for the Preliminary Grade examination.

Major chords

Minor chords

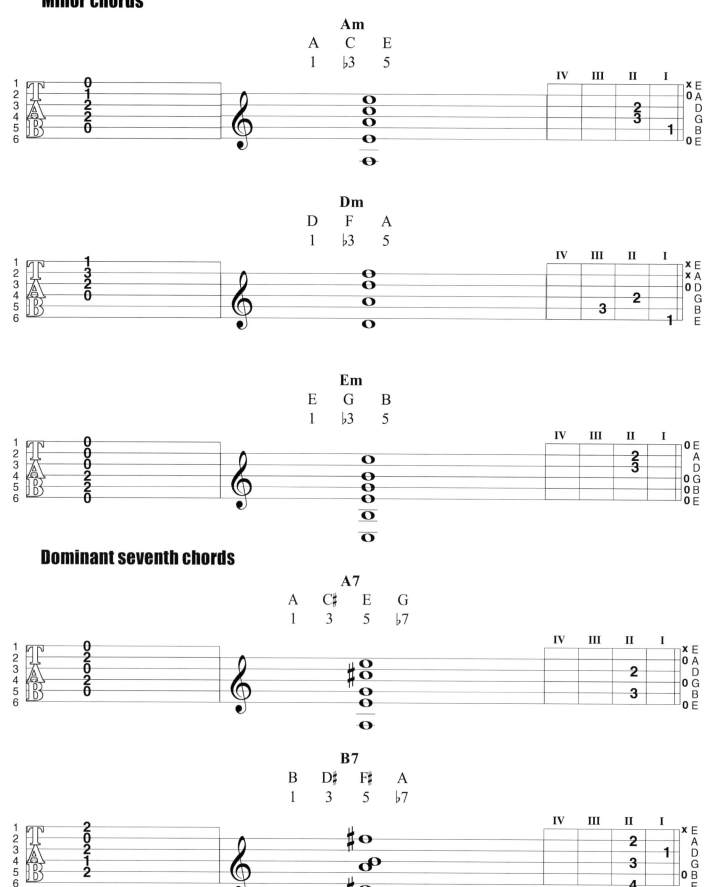

Dominant seventh chords

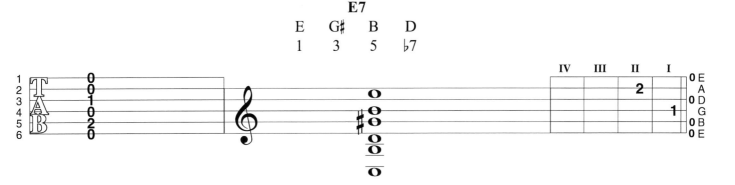

INFORMATION AND ADVICE

A maximum of 12 marks may be awarded in this section of the examination.

The examiner may request you to play any of the required chords from memory. Each chord should be played once only using a single downstroke. Make sure that your fingers are carefully and correctly positioned before playing the chord. Ensure that you use the *tips* of your fretting-hand fingers and that no required open strings are muted. Press as close to the fretwire as possible to aid clarity and minimise fret buzz.

In the fingerboard diagrams, strings which should be omitted are marked by an X – so be careful not to strike these strings when playing the chord.

Rhythm playing

In this section of the examination, the candidate will be shown a chord chart and will be allowed a short time (of about 30 seconds) to study it before being asked to play it. The chord chart will contain only chords listed in Section 2 of this book. Some examples of the *type* of chart that may be presented at this grade are given below. The tempo markings are intended only as broad guidelines.

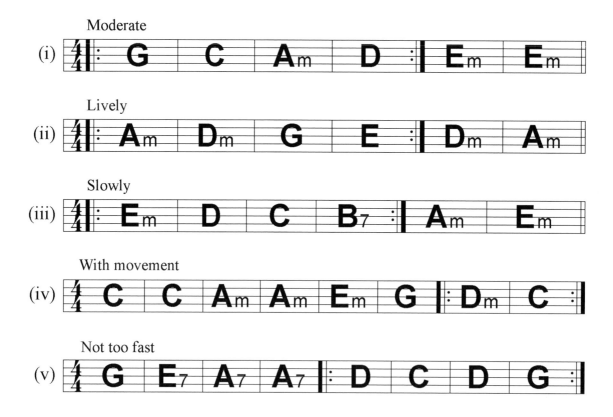

In practice, musicians may write out chord charts not only on staves (as shown above) but sometimes chords are written above staves instead, or quite commonly just with bar lines (as in the example below). In the examination, to achieve maximum visual clarity, all chord charts will be presented in the style shown below.

INFORMATION AND ADVICE

At this grade the time signature is limited to $\frac{4}{4}$ time, although this does not necessarily mean that candidates should restrict themselves to merely four strums per bar: whilst the time signature should be evident by maintaining a regular pulse and even tempo, with no unnecessary slowing (particularly at bar lines), the more imaginative the rhythm playing is – the higher the mark that may be achieved. The musical style that is used is left to the discretion of the candidate. Fingerpicking can be used, rather than strumming, if preferred by the candidate.

After playing the first chord chart candidates may, at the examiner's discretion, be given an additional chart to play. This will be of a similar difficulty to the first one.

Gaining marks

A maximum of 30 marks may be awarded in this section of the examination.

Marks are awarded for accuracy of chords: apart from ensuring that the fretting hand has fingered the correct frets and strings, candidates should also pay attention to the striking of strings with the strumming hand. For example, be particularly careful not to strum the 6th string on B7 or on all D chords.

Chord changes should be as smooth and fluid as possible and lack any sense of hesitation. Chords should ring clear, i.e. free of fret buzz or the unintended muting of notes with the fretting-hand fingers.

During the time given to look over the chord chart, candidates should try to discover the overall structure of the progression. At this grade, the only indications on the chart other than the time signature and tempo are repeat marks. Passages to be repeated are indicated by two vertical dots at the start and end of the section to be repeated.

For example:

 should be played as:

RHYTHM PLAYING TIPS

Strumming hand

- It will aid fluency of rhythm playing if the strumming hand pivots from the wrist; a fluid and easy strumming action is best achieved this way, with the wrist loose and relaxed.

- If the wrist is stiff and not allowed to move freely then excessive arm movement will occur as the strumming action will be forced to come from the elbow instead. As this can never move as fluently as the wrist action there will be a loss of smoothness and rhythmic potential.

Fretting hand

- Be careful not to overgrip with the fretting-hand thumb on the back of the guitar neck as this will cause muscle fatigue and tend to limit freedom of the thumb to move.

- It is essential that the fretting-hand thumb is allowed to move freely when changing chords. If the thumb remains static this restricts the optimum positioning of the fingers for the next chord, which may result in unnecessary stretching and the involuntary dampening of certain strings (as the fingers are not positioned upright on their tips).

- For the fingers to move freely, the wrist, elbow and shoulder must be flexible and relaxed: try to ensure that this is not inhibited by your standing or sitting position.

Lead playing

In this section of the examination, the candidate will be shown a chord progression containing chords chosen from those listed in Section 2 of this book. The examiner will then play this progression (either live or recorded) and the candidate should improvise over this using an appropriate scale selected from Section 1 of this book.

Some examples of the *type* of chord chart that will be presented at this grade are shown below. The scale suggestions are given for guidance in this book, but will NOT appear in the examination.

(i) The C major scale could be used to improvise over the following progression...

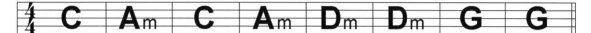

(ii) The A natural minor scale could be used to improvise over the following progression...

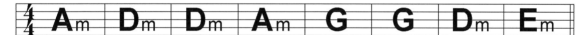

(iii) The E blues scale could be used to improvise over the following progression...

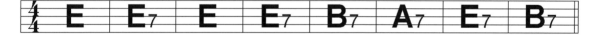

(iv) The G pentatonic major scale could be used to improvise over the following progression...

INFORMATION AND ADVICE

The progression will be played a total of three times. During the first playing the candidate should not play, but rather listen and digest the sequence, before improvising over the next two cycles. After playing the final sequence the examiner will end on the tonic (i.e. first) chord of the key.

To ensure accuracy it is essential that the candidate selects the most appropriate scale to improvise with. The examiner will NOT advise on this. At this grade the starting chord of each sequence will always be the key chord. The table that follows provides a summary of when to use each scale.

Starting Chord	Key	Scale to be used
C	C major	C major
G	G major	G pentatonic major
Am	A minor	A natural minor
E or E7	E blues	E blues

At the examiner's discretion, an additional sequence may be selected for the candidate to improvise over. Although this will again contain chords only from Section 2 of this book, the candidate may need to select a different scale from Section 1 to improvise with.

Gaining marks

A maximum of 30 marks may be awarded in this section of the examination.

Whilst you will need to select a scale to improvise with, be aware that the purpose of the scale is essentially to set the series of notes that will be in tune in a particular key and is not an end in itself. Endeavour to make your improvisation melodically and rhythmically inventive and imaginative rather than sounding scale-like.

The style of lead playing should enhance and empathise with the chordal accompaniment, which may be from a range of musical styles such as rock, pop and blues. Playing should be fluent but without the need for speed for its own sake; more important is the overall musical effect that is achieved.

LEAD PLAYING TIPS

Phrasing

- Try to create interesting melodic and rhythmic phrases within your improvisation.

- Avoid the inappropriate use of continuous scalic playing by not being afraid to leave gaps between, and within, phrases.

Resolving notes

- When improvising from a scale you will find that some notes sound better, and more 'resolved', against certain chords than others. However, as long as you stay within the scale, no notes will be 'out of tune'. If you play a note that sounds 'unresolved' against a particular chord, simply move up or down one note within the scale.

- Rest assured that none of the notes from the correct scale will totally clash with the backing chords; let your ears guide you as to which scale notes sound best over particular chords.

Improvising blues

- When playing the E Blues scale, be careful not to over emphasise the B♭ note (3rd fret G string): this is meant to be used only as a 'passing note'. You can certainly play this note, but it's best not to start, or linger, on it.

Spoken tests

A maximum of 10 marks may be awarded in this section of the examination.

FINGERBOARD KNOWLEDGE

In this section of the examination the candidate may be asked to name any note from the scales in Section 1 – so that when the examiner names a particular string and fret the candidate should be able to quickly identify this note (which will be chosen from one of the required scales). In order to establish a solid musical foundation it is important that candidates are aware of the notes that they are playing rather than merely duplicating finger patterns.

The names of the notes contained in each scale are shown above the guitarographs in Section 1 of this book. A summary is given below.

String	Fret 0	1	2	3
5	A		B	C
4	D		E	F
3	G		A	B♭
2	B	C		D
1	E			G

KNOWLEDGE OF THE INSTRUMENT

Candidates should have a basic knowledge of the instrument. In particular:

(i)   The names of the strings

thickest string —

6th string	E
5th string	A
4th string	D
3rd string	G
2nd string	B
1st string	E

thinnest string —

(ii)   Basic information about the anatomy of the candidate's guitar – in particular, the location of:

- the machine heads (tuning heads)

- the nut

- the bridge

- the pick-ups

- the pick-up selector

- the volume and tone controls (if appropriate).

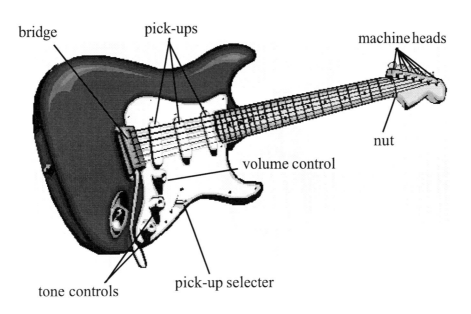

Aural assessments

A maximum of 10 marks may be awarded in total during this section of the examination. The candidate will be given a selection of the following tests, which will include a rhythm test and at least two other tests.

REPETITION OF RHYTHMS

The examiner will twice tap, or play (on a single note), a 2 bar rhythm in $\frac{4}{4}$ time. The candidate should then attempt to reproduce this rhythm by clapping, tapping or playing. Some examples of the *type* of rhythm are given below. Note that the first bar will contain a combination of two quarter notes (crotchets) and four eighth notes (quavers), whilst the second bar will consist of a whole note (semibreve).

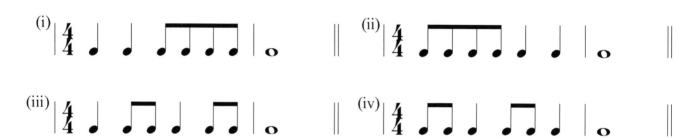

REPETITION OF MELODIC PHRASES

The candidate will be asked to look away while the examiner plays a one bar phrase in $\frac{4}{4}$ time. This will consist of adjacent notes taken from a scale listed in Section 1 of this book. The candidate will be told which scale is to be used, and the keynote will be played. The phrase will consist of quarter notes (crotchets) and eighth notes (quavers) – but eighth notes will only occur on notes of the same pitch.

The examiner will play the phrase twice before the candidate makes a first attempt to reproduce the phrase on the guitar. If required, the examiner will play the phrase one further time prior to the candidate's second attempt. Some examples of the *type* of phrase are shown below.

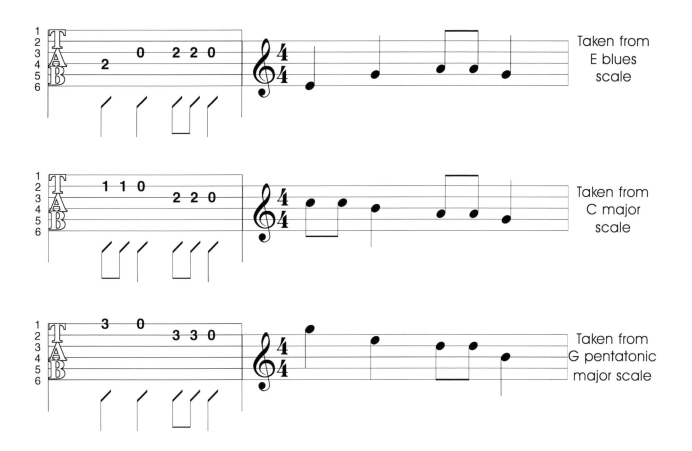

Taken from
E blues
scale

Taken from
C major
scale

Taken from
G pentatonic
major scale

KEEPING TIME

The examiner will twice play a simple four bar melody in $\frac{4}{4}$ time. During the second playing the candidate should clap the main pulse, accenting the first beat of each bar. Two examples are shown, in both standard notation and tablature.

Examiner plays:

Candidate claps:

Examiner plays:

Candidate claps:

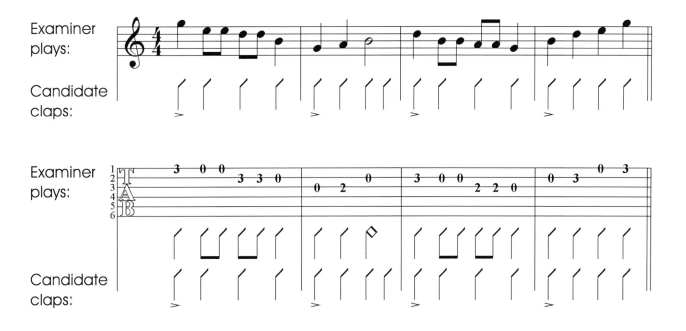

PITCH TEST

While the candidate looks away the examiner will play two notes consecutively, with a short gap in-between. Both notes will be taken from the C major scale and will be no more than a perfect fifth apart. The candidate will then be asked to identify which one was the highest – i.e. the note that was played first, or the note that was played last.

Example:

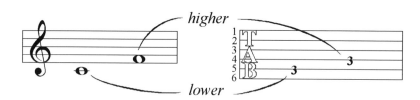

HARMONY TEST

While the candidate looks away, the examiner will play a short chord progression containing either all major chords or all minor chords. The candidate will then be asked whether the progression consisted of major or minor chords. Here are two examples:

(i) *major* | G | C | G | C | G ‖

(ii) *minor* | Em | Am | Em | Am | Em ‖

RGT
Registry of Guitar Tutors

EXAMINATION ENTRY FORM
ELECTRIC GUITAR
PRELIMINARY GRADE

ONLINE ENTRY – AVAILABLE FOR UK CANDIDATES ONLY

For **UK candidates**, entries and payments can be made online at www.RGT.org, using the entry code below. You will be able to pay the entry fee by credit or debit card at a secure payment page on the website.

Your unique and confidential examination entry code is:

EP-0398-BI

Keep this unique code confidential, as it can only be used once. Once you have entered online, you should sign this form overleaf. **You must bring this signed form to your exam and hand it to the examiner in order to be admitted to the exam room.**

If NOT entering online, please complete BOTH sides of this form and return to the address overleaf.

SESSION (Spring/Summer/Winter): _____   YEAR: _____

Dates/times NOT available: _____

Note: Only name *specific* dates (and times on those dates) when it would be *absolutely impossible* for you to attend due to important prior commitments (such as pre-booked overseas travel) which cannot be cancelled. We will then endeavour to avoid scheduling an exam session in your area on those dates. In fairness to all other candidates in your area, **only list dates on which it would be impossible for you to attend.** An entry form that blocks out unreasonable periods may be returned. (Exams may be held on any day of the week including, but not exclusively, weekends. Exams may be held within or outside of the school term.)

Candidate Details: *Please write as clearly as possible using BLOCK CAPITALS*

Candidate Name (as to appear on certificate): _____

Address: _____

_____ Postcode: _____

Tel. No. (day): _____ (evening): _____

(mobile): _____ Email: _____

Teacher Details *(if applicable)*

Teacher Name (as to appear on certificate): _____

RGT Tutor Code (if applicable): _____

Address: _____

_____ Postcode: _____

Tel. No. (day): _____ (evening): _____

(mobile): _____ Email: _____

RGT Electric Guitar Official Entry Form

The standard LCM entry form is NOT valid for Electric Guitar exam entries.
Entry to the examination is only possible via this original form.
Photocopies of this form will not be accepted under *any* circumstances.

- Completion of this entry form is an agreement to comply with the current syllabus requirements and conditions of entry published at www.RGT.org. Where candidates are entered for examinations by a teacher, parent or guardian that person hereby takes responsibility that the candidate is entered in accordance with the current syllabus requirements and conditions of entry.
- If you are being taught by an *RGT registered* tutor, please hand this completed form to your tutor and request him/her to administer the entry on your behalf.
- For candidates with special needs, a letter giving details should be attached.

Examination Fee: £__________________ Late Entry Fee (if applicable): £____________________

Total amount submitted: £_________________

Cheques or postal orders should be made payable to Registry of Guitar Tutors.

Details of conditions of entry, entry deadlines and examination fees are obtainable from the RGT website: www.RGT.org

Once an entry has been accepted, entry fees cannot be refunded.

CANDIDATE INFORMATION (UK Candidates only)

In order to meet our obligations in monitoring the implementation of equal opportunities policies, UK candidates are required to supply the information requested below. *The information provided will in no way whatsoever influence the marks awarded during the examination.*

Date of birth: ________________ Age: ________ Gender – please circle: male / female

Ethnicity (please enter 2 digit code from chart below): ______ Signed: ____________________

ETHNIC ORIGIN CLASSIFICATIONS (If you prefer not to say, write '17' in the space above.)

White: **01 British** **02 Irish** **03 Other white background**

Mixed: **04 White & black Caribbean** **05 White & black African** **06 White & Asian** **07 Other mixed background**

Asian or Asian British: **08 Indian** **09 Pakistani** **10 Bangladeshi** **11 Other Asian background**

Black or Black British: **12 Caribbean** **13 African** **14 Other black background**

Chinese or Other Ethnic Group: **15 Chinese** **16 Other** **17 Prefer not to say**

I understand and accept the current syllabus regulations and conditions of entry for this examination as specified on the RGT website.

Signed by candidate (if aged 18 or over) ___________________________ Date _____________

If candidate is under 18, this form should be signed by a parent/guardian/teacher (circle which applies):

Signed ______________________ Name_____________________________ Date_____________

UK ENTRIES

See overleaf for details of how to enter online OR return this form to:

Registry of Guitar Tutors, Registry Mews, 11 to 13 Wilton Road, Bexhill-on-Sea, E. Sussex, TN40 1HY

(If you have submitted your entry online do NOT post this form, instead you need to sign it above and hand it to the examiner on the day of your exam.)

To contact the RGT office telephone 01424 222222 or Email office@RGT.org

NON-UK ENTRIES

To locate the address within your country that entry forms should be sent to, and to view exam fees in your currency, visit the RGT website **www.RGT.org** and navigate to the 'RGT Worldwide' section.